My First
CATECHISM

Rev. Lawrence G. Lovasik, S.V.D.
Divine World Missionary

CATHOLIC BOOK
PUBLISHING CORP.
New Jersey

CPSIA   May 2018   10 9 8 7 6 5 4 3 2   L/P

NIHIL OBSTAT: Daniel V. Flynn, J.C.D., *Censor Librorum*
IMPRIMATUR: ✝ Joseph T. O'Keefe, *Vicar General, Archdiocese of New York*
© 1983 Catholic Book Publishing Corp., N.J.—Printed in China   ISBN 978-0-89942-382-1

1. WHY I AM IN THE WORLD

1. Who made you?

God made me.

2. Why did God make you?

God made me because He is good
and He wants me to be happy
with Him in heaven.

Jesus speaks to us
through His Church.

3. What do you have to do to be happy with God in heaven?

To be happy with God in heaven,
I must know about God,
I must love God,
and I must do what God wants me to do.

The Holy Family
teaches us how
to love and serve
God.

4. How do you know what God wants you to do?

Jesus tells me what God wants me to do through the Catholic Church.

5. How do you show your love for God?

I show my love for God when I pray
and go to Holy Mass,
when I obey God,
and when I love everyone for the love of God.

People give God the highest worship at Holy Mass.

6. How do you serve God?

I serve God when I keep God's commandments
and the laws of the Catholic Church,
and when I help others.

Jesus helps His foster-father Joseph.

3

2. GOD

7. Who is God?

God is the highest Being because He made everything.

God made all things from nothing. He also made man.

8. What does the Catholic Church teach you about God?

The Catholic Church teaches me
that God is the highest Good.
He always was and always will be.
He knows all things.
He can do all things.
He is everywhere.
He sees me and cares for me.

9. **Since God is the highest Good what should you do?**

    Since God is the highest Good
    I should love Him with all my heart,
    above anything else in the world,
    and I should worship Him.

10. **How do you worship God?**

    I worship God by going to Mass on Sunday
    and by saying prayers.

11. What must you believe about God?

I must believe that there is only one God, and that there are three Persons in God.

The three Persons in God are: the Father, the Son, and the Holy Spirit.

12. Who are the three Persons in God?

The three Persons in God are:
the Father, the Son, and the Holy Spirit.

13. What is the Blessed Trinity?

The Blessed Trinity is one God
in three Divine Persons.

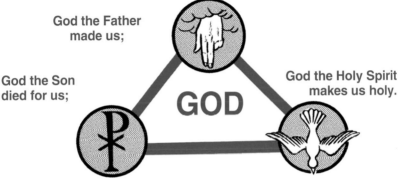

God the Father made us;

God the Son died for us;

GOD

God the Holy Spirit makes us holy.

14. Who told us about the Blessed Trinity?

Jesus, the Son of God, told us about the
Blessed Trinity.

15. How do you show your faith in the Blessed Trinity?

I show my faith in the Blessed Trinity
when I make the Sign of the Cross.

16. What do you say when you make the Sign of the Cross?

When I make the Sign of the Cross I say:
In the name of the Father, and of the Son,
and of the Holy Spirit. Amen.

4. CREATION

17. Why do we call God the Creator?

We call God the Creator
because He made all things from nothing.

God made the earth, the sky and the sea.

18. Who made the angels?

God made the angels.

19. What is an angel?

An angel is a spirit, without a body.

20. Who are the good angels?

The good angels obeyed God
and are now happy with him in heaven.

21. How do the good angels help us?

The good angels help us by praying for us
and by taking care of us.

God made the angels to honor Him and protect us.

22. Who is your Guardian Angel?

My Guardian Angel is the good angel that
God gave me to take care of me
and to help me to be good.

23. Who are the devils?

The devils are the bad angels
who did not want to obey God,
so God punished them in hell.

24. Who made man?

God made man.

25. Who is man?

Man is a creature of God with a body and a soul.

26. Who were the first man and woman?

Adam and Eve, our first parents, were the first man and woman.

God made Adam and Eve, our first parents.

27. How did Adam and Eve sin?

Adam and Eve sinned
by eating of the fruit of a certain tree
that grew in the Garden of Paradise.

28. What happened when Adam and Eve sinned?

When Adam and Eve sinned
they lost God's grace
and the right to heaven.

29. How did God punish Adam and Eve?

God punished Adam and Eve
by sending them from the Garden of Paradise
to work, suffer, and die on earth.

An angel sent Adam and Eve from Paradise.

30. What happened to us on account of Adam's sin?

On account of Adam's sin
we come into the world without grace.

31. What did God promise Adam and Eve?

God promised Adam and Eve to send into the
world a Savior.

5. GOD THE SON

32. Who is the Savior of all people?

Jesus Christ is the Savior of all people.

33. What does the Catholic Church teach about Jesus Christ?

The Catholic Church teaches
that Jesus Christ is God made man.

34. Is Jesus Christ only one Person?

Jesus Christ is only one Person —
the second Person of the Blessed Trinity.

35. When did the Son of God become man?

The Son of God became man
after the Blessed Virgin Mary said "yes" to God
when He asked her to be the Mother of His Son.

The Angel Gabriel asks Mary to be the Mother of God.

12

36. How did the Son of God become man?

The Son of God became man of the Virgin
   Mary
by the power of the Holy Spirit.

37. When was Jesus Christ born?

Jesus Christ was born of the Virgin Mary
on Christmas Day,
more than two thousand years ago.

Jesus is born in Bethlehem.

38. Why is Jesus Christ both God and man?

Jesus Christ is both God and man
because He is the Son of God
and the Son of the Virgin Mary.

Children should
pray to the
Infant Jesus.

13

39. Why is Jesus Christ our Redeemer?

Jesus Christ is our Redeemer
because He offered His sufferings to God
to make up for our sins,
to bring us God's grace,
and to buy heaven back for us.

Jesus died on the cross to save us
from sin and the devil.

40. What made Jesus suffer and die for us?

Jesus suffered and died for us
because He loved His heavenly Father
and because He loved us.

41. What does the Resurrection of Jesus mean?

The Resurrection of Jesus means that Jesus
came back to life again on Easter Sunday,
the third day after His death.

Jesus rose from the dead that
we may live forever.

42. Why did Jesus rise from the dead?

Jesus rose from the dead
to show that He is true God,
and that we also will rise again.

43. When did Jesus go back to heaven?

Jesus went back to heaven on Ascension
Day, forty days after His Resurrection.

44. When will Jesus come again?

Jesus will come again to judge everyone
on the last day.

6. GOD THE HOLY SPIRIT

45. Who is the Holy Spirit?

The Holy Spirit is God,
the Third Person of the Blessed Trinity.

46. When did Jesus and His Father send the Holy Spirit?

Jesus and His Father sent the Holy Spirit
to the Church on Pentecost—
fifty days after Jesus rose from the dead.

The Holy Spirit came upon the Blessed Virgin Mary and the Apostles.

47. What does the Holy Spirit do for you?

The Holy Spirit makes my soul holy
through the gift of His grace.

48. What is grace?

Grace is a gift of God
that makes my soul holy and pleasing to
God, and helps me to live as a child of God.

49. How does grace make you holy and pleasing to God?

Grace makes me holy and pleasing to God because it helps me to believe in God, to hope in
God, and to love God.

50. How does God's grace help you to live as a child of God?

God's grace helps me to live as a child of
God because it gives light to my mind and
strength to my will to do good and to avoid
evil.

Jesus lives in our soul by giving us His grace.

51. How does the Holy Spirit give you grace?

The Holy Spirit gives me grace when I
receive the Sacraments
and when I pray and do kind things.

7. THE CATHOLIC CHURCH

52. What is the Catholic Church?

The Catholic Church is the union
of all baptized persons
under the Holy Father, the Pope.

53. What do the people in the Catholic Church have?

The people in the Catholic Church have
the same true faith,
the same Sacrifice of the Mass,
and the same Sacraments.

54. Why did Jesus start the Church?

Jesus started the Church to lead all people
to heaven.

55. How did Jesus start the Church?

Jesus started the Church by picking twelve
Apostles
who were always with Him.

Jesus sent His Apostles to
spread His Church in the
whole world.

56. What power did Jesus give His Apostles?

Jesus gave His Apostles the power to teach, to make people holy, and to guide them to God.

57. To whom did Jesus give special power?

Jesus gave special power to St. Peter by making him the head of the Apostles and the chief teacher and ruler of the Church.

58. Who takes the place of St. Peter today?

The Holy Father, the Bishop of Rome, takes the place of St. Peter today.

The Holy Father in Rome takes the place of Jesus and St. Peter.

59. Who takes the place of the Apostles today?

The bishops of the Church take the place of the Apostles today.

60. Who helps the bishops take care of God's People?

The priests help the bishops to take care of God's People.

61. What did Jesus give His Church?

Jesus gave His Church the truths of faith and the seven Sacraments.

8. THE SEVEN SACRAMENTS

62. What is a Sacrament?

A Sacrament is a holy sign
by which Jesus gives us His grace.

63. What are the seven Sacraments?

The seven Sacraments are: Baptism, Confirmation, Holy Eucharist, Penance, Anointing of the Sick, Holy Orders, and Matrimony.

64. Why did Jesus give the Sacraments to the Catholic Church?

Jesus gave the Sacraments to the Catholic Church
to give us grace.

Jesus lives in the People of God through the grace of the Sacraments.

65. What does grace do for us?

Grace makes our soul holy and pleasing to God.

66. How does grace help us lead a good life?

Grace helps us to lead a good life
because it gives light to our mind
and strength to our will
to do good and to avoid evil.

67. What is Baptism?

Baptism is a new birth as a child of God,
the beginning of a new life
of God's grace in us.

We become children
of God in baptism.

68. What is Confirmation?

Confirmation is the Sacrament
by which those born again in Baptism
receive now the Holy Spirit,
the gift of the Father and the Son.

68. What does Jesus do for you in Confirmation?

In Confirmation Jesus sends the Holy
Spirit to me again
and gives me new strength
to live a Christian life.

70. What is the Holy Eucharist?

The Holy Eucharist is Jesus Christ
after the bread and wine have been changed
into His Body and Blood at Mass.

This is My Body...
This is My Blood

Jesus becomes present in
the bread and wine at Mass.

71. What does Jesus do in the Mass?

In the Mass Jesus gives Himself to His
Father as He did on the cross,
but He does not suffer anymore.

72. What does Jesus give you in Holy Communion?

In Holy Communion Jesus gives me Himself as food for my soul.

Jesus comes to us
as our food
in Holy Communion.

73. What does Jesus do for you in the Sacrament of Penance?

In the Sacrament of Penance Jesus forgives my sins
and gives me grace to be a better Catholic.

Jesus takes away our sins in the Sacrament of Penance.

74. What does Jesus do in the Anointing of the Sick?

In the Anointing of the Sick Jesus gives His grace to the sick and to old people.

75. What does Jesus do in Holy Orders?

In Holy Orders Jesus gives us priests
to teach us, to offer Holy Mass
and to take away our sins.

76. What does Jesus do in Matrimony?

In Matrimony Jesus comes to a man and woman to make them one in holy marriage and to bless them.

9. PRAYER

77. What do you do when you pray?

When I pray I talk to God and He talks to me.

78. What do you tell God when you pray?

When I pray I tell God that I adore Him as
  my God,
that I thank Him for all He does for me,
that I beg Him to forgive all my sins,
and that I ask Him to help me and other
  people.

79. For whom should you pray?

I should pray for my mother and father,
for my brothers and sisters and friends,
for my priests and teachers,
for the Catholic Church,
and for those who have died.

We should pray
often every day.

80. When should you pray?

I should pray in the morning and at night,
before and after meals, when I need God's
help, at Holy Mass and anytime I want to
  think of God.

81. Do you pray to anyone else besides God?

I pray to the Blessed Virgin Mary
because she is the Mother of God and my
Mother. I pray to the Saints and to my
Guardian Angel.

10. THE TEN COMMANDMENTS

God gave Moses the Ten Commandments on Mount Sinai.

82. What are the Ten Commandments?

The Ten Commandments are:
1. I, the Lord, am your God,
   you shall not have other gods besides Me.
2. You shall not take the name of the Lord,
   your God, in vain.
3. Remember to keep holy the sabbath day.
4. Honor your father and your mother.
5. You shall not kill.
6. You shall not commit adultery.
7. You shall not steal.
8. You shall not bear false witness against
   your neighbor.
9. You shall not covet your neighbor's wife.
10. You shall not covet anything that belongs
    to your neighbor.

THE DUTIES OF CATHOLICS

83. What are the duties of Catholics?

The duties of Catholics are:
1. To go to Mass every Sunday and Holy day of obligation.
2. To receive the Sacrament of the Eucharist and Penance.
3. To study the Catholic religion.
4. To keep the marriage laws of the Church.
5. To help the Catholic Church.
6. To help the missions.

Catholics all over the world have the same duties.

11. SIN

Jesus teaches us through His Church
to keep the commandments and to avoid sin.

84. When do you commit a sin?

I commit a sin when I disobey God.

85. How do you know what God wants you to do?

I know what God wants me to do in the
Ten Commandments He gave us.

86. What does God tell you in the Ten Commandments?

In the Ten Commandments God tells me to
love Him with all my heart
and to love people for His sake.

87. Will God forgive all your sins?

God will forgive all my sins if I am really sorry for them.

88. What do I say in the Act of Contrition?

In the Act of Contrition I tell God
that I am very sorry that I have offended
Him because I love Him,
and that I hate all my sins
and promise to try never to sin again.

89. Why should you be really sorry for your sins?

I should be really sorry for my sins because they displease God, who is all-good, and because they made Jesus suffer on the cross.

We should be sorry for our sins because they made Jesus suffer on the cross.

PRAYERS TO REMEMBER

OUR FATHER

OUR Father, Who art in heaven,
hallowed be Thy name;
Thy kingdom come,
Thy will be done on earth as it is in heaven.
Give us this day our daily bread,
and forgive us our trespasses,
as we forgive those
who trespass against us;
and lead us not into temptation,
but deliver us from evil. Amen.

HAIL MARY

HAIL Mary, full of grace,
the Lord is with thee;
blessed art thou among women,
and blessed is the fruit of thy womb, Jesus.

Holy Mary, Mother of God,
pray for us sinners,
now and at the hour of our death. Amen.

PRAISE TO GOD

GLORY be to the Father, and to the Son,
and to the Holy Spirit,
as it was in the beginning,
is now, and ever shall be,
world without end. Amen.

THE APOSTLES' CREED

I BELIEVE in <u>God</u>,
the Father <u>almighty</u>,
Creator of heaven and earth,
and in <u>Jesus Christ</u>, His only Son, our Lord,
Who was conceived by the Holy Spirit,
born of the Virgin Mary,
suffered under Pontius Pilate,
was crucified, died and was buried;
He descended into hell;
on the third day He rose again from the dead;
He ascended into heaven,
and is seated at the right hand of God the
   Father almighty;
from there He will come to judge the living and
   the dead.

I believe in the <u>Holy</u> Spirit,
the holy catholic Church,
the communion of saints,
the forgiveness of sins,
the resurrection of the body,
and life everlasting. Amen.

FAITH, HOPE, AND LOVE

I BELIEVE in You, my God,
because You are the eternal Truth.

I HOPE in You, my God,
because You are merciful, faithful and powerful.

I LOVE You, my God,
because You are all-good and loving,
and I love all people for love of You.

ACT OF CONTRITION

O MY God, I am heartily sorry
for having offended You,
and I detest all my sins,
because of Your just punishments,
but most of all because they offend You,
my God,
Who are all good
and deserving of all my love.
I firmly resolve,
with the help of Your grace,
to sin no more and to avoid
the near occasions of sin.

TO THE HOLY FAMILY

J ESUS, Mary and Joseph, I give you my heart and
my soul.
Jesus, Mary and Joseph, help me in my last agony.
Jesus, Mary and Joseph, may I breathe forth my soul
in peace with you.

TO MY GUARDIAN ANGEL

A NGEL of God, my Guardian dear,
God's love for me has sent you here;
ever this day be at my side,
to light and guard, to rule and guide. Amen.